# 10 EASTER HYM

## VOLUME 2

- ARE YOU WASHED IN THE BLOOD?
- DOWN AT THE CROSS
- HE LIVES (I KNOW THAT MY REDEEMER LIVES!)
- JESUS SAVES
- O SACRED HEAD, NOW WOUNDED
- O THE BLOOD OF JESUS
- TELL ME THE STORY OF JESUS
- THE OLD RUGGED CROSS
- THERE IS A FOUNTAIN
- WHEN I SURVEY THE WONDROUS CROSS

## ARRANGED BY B. C. DOCKERY

# Are You Washed in the Blood?

Elisha A. Hoffman
arr. B. C. Dockery

# Down at the Cross

John H. Stockton
arr. B. C. Dockery

# He Lives
## (I Know That My Redeemer Lives!)

Samuel Medley
arr. B. C. Dockery

# Jesus Saves

## We Have Heard the Joyful Sound

William J. Kirkpatrick
arr. B. C. Dockery

Jesus Saves

# O Sacred Head, Now Wounded

Hans Leo Hassler; harmonized by J. S. Bach

arr. B. C. Dockery

# O the Blood

Traditional
arr. B. C. Dockery

# Tell Me the Story of Jesus

John R. Sweney
arr. B. C. Dockery

# The Old Rugged Cross

George Bennard
arr. B. C. Dockery

# There Is a Fountain

Traditional
arr. B. C. Dockery

There Is a Fountain

# When I Survey the Wondrous Cross

Lowell Mason
arr. B. C. Dockery

# Are You Washed in the Blood?

Elisha A. Hoffman
arr. B. C. Dockery

Flute 1

# Are You Washed in the Blood?

Elisha A. Hoffman
arr. B. C. Dockery

Flute 1

# Down at the Cross

John H. Stockton
arr. B. C. Dockery

# Down at the Cross

Piano

John H. Stockton
arr. B. C. Dockery

# He Lives
## (I Know That My Redeemer Lives!)

Flute 1

Samuel Medley
arr. B. C. Dockery

# He Lives
## (I Know That My Redeemer Lives!)

Piano

Samuel Medley
arr. B. C. Dockery

# Jesus Saves
## We Have Heard the Joyful Sound

William J. Kirkpatrick
arr. B. C. Dockery

# Jesus Saves
## We Have Heard the Joyful Sound

William J. Kirkpatrick
arr. B. C. Dockery

# O Sacred Head, Now Wounded

Hans Leo Hassler; harmonized by J. S. Bach

arr. B. C. Dockery

Flute 1

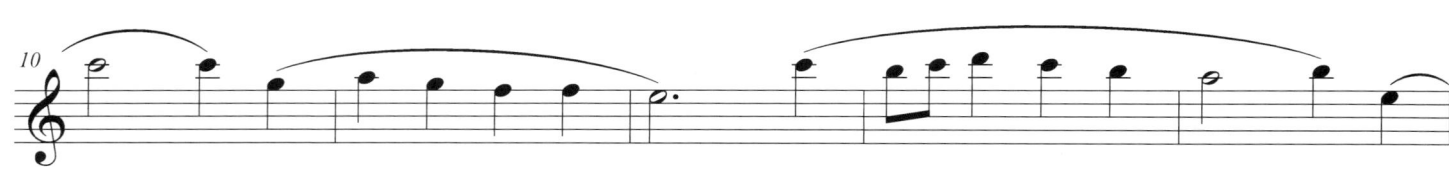

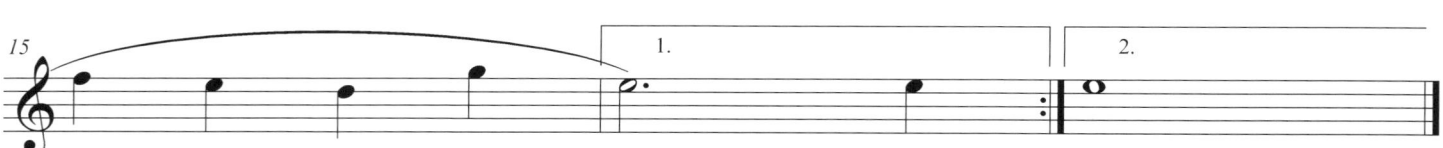

# O Sacred Head, Now Wounded

Hans Leo Hassler; harmonized by J. S. Bach

arr. B. C. Dockery

# O the Blood

Traditional
arr. B. C. Dockery

# O the Blood

Traditional
arr. B. C. Dockery

# Tell Me the Story of Jesus

John R. Sweney
arr. B. C. Dockery

Flute 1

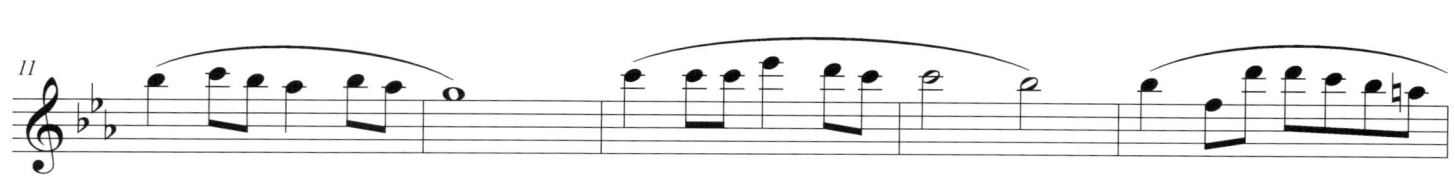

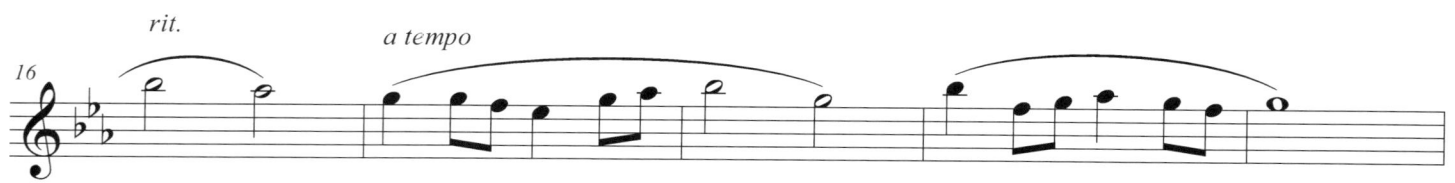

# Tell Me the Story of Jesus

John R. Sweney
arr. B. C. Dockery

# The Old Rugged Cross

George Bennard
arr. B. C. Dockery

# The Old Rugged Cross

Piano

George Bennard
arr. B. C. Dockery

# There Is a Fountain

Flute 1

Traditional
arr. B. C. Dockery

# There Is a Fountain

Piano

Traditional
arr. B. C. Dockery

# When I Survey the Wondrous Cross

Flute 1

Lowell Mason
arr. B. C. Dockery

# When I Survey the Wondrous Cross

Piano

Lowell Mason
arr. B. C. Dockery

Made in the USA
Columbia, SC
03 March 2025

54667986R00026